I
Want To
Look
For Bugs

Sheila Marcotte

illustrated by Aleksandra Maslova

I Want to Look for Bugs

Printed in the United States of America

A 2 Z Press LLC

PO Box 582

Deleon Springs, FL 32130

terriesizemorestoryteller.com

sizemore3630@aol.com

440-241-3126

ISBN: 978-1-946908-77-3

Dedication

For Helen,
Who loves art
and dance and giving hugs,
May you always find
time to look for bugs....

I want to look for bugs and things,

Like butterflies and
stuff with wings.

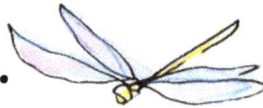

I want to catch
them

in my hand,

I want to look for bugs.

I will look for bugs with you,

Together we can

find a few.

Like moths and ants and worms or slugs,

I will help you look for bugs.

I want to see

grasshoppers play,

And watch a praying mantis pray.

Why does

the lady bug

fly away?

I want to look for bugs.

We'll press our faces to the grass,

And watch an earthworm slowly pass.

Then gather
June bugs
in a glass,

I'll help you look for bugs.

We'll count the legs of a centipede,

For butterflies, a net we'll need.

Then learn how long
an inch worm is,

When we look for bugs.

When twilight's blanket
dims the skies,

We can catch some fireflies.

Then watch them glow before our eyes,

When we catch some bugs.

But after we've
had all that fun,

And when the day is almost done,

Remember each and every one,

Of the bugs we found.

Promise that you won't keep some,

And put them back where they came from.

So that the next time when I come,

We can look for bugs.

Glossary of Bugs

<u>Ants</u> - Ants are members of the insect world. There are over 10,000 types of ants! They do not have ears but instead can feel vibrations through their feet to detect sound. Ants are social insects that live in colonies with as many as one million other ants. Single ants can lift up to 20 times their own weight!

Butterfly - A Butterfly is an insect that can be found all over the world. It has a four-stage life cycle and transforms from a caterpillar to a butterfly. They have transparent wings, that are usually very colorful, and they taste with their feet!

Centipede - The centipede is a multi-legged creature that has one pair of legs per body section. Despite the name, a centipede can have any where from 30 – 354 legs. There is estimated to be over 8000 species in existence worldwide.

<u>Earthworm</u> -An Earthworm can grow to be a few inches long and dwells in soil or moist leaf litter. As they borrow in the dirt they also eat the soil then release it in the form of a nutrient.

<u>Firefly</u> - The Firefly, also called a Lightening Bug, is actually a member of the beetle family. A reaction of enzymes in their body creates their abdomen area to glow or "light" up. Naturally attracted to moisture, the Firefly can often be seen lighting up the night when it rains.

Grasshopper - The grasshopper is an insect that has 6 legs, 2 antennae and 2 sets of wings. They have very powerful hind legs that allow them to jump sometimes as much as 3 feet high and 9 feet in distance!

Inchworm - An inchworm is not a worm but actually a caterpillar and a member of the moth family. They average in size to be about one inch long but can come in many different colors. They have feet on the front and back end of their body that causes them to form a loop of their body when they move.

June Bug - The June bug is a member of the beetle family. They have two sets of wings, but are not very good flyers. A June bug can live under- ground for up to 3 years and loves to munch on the roots of grass. They are hopelessly at- tracted to lights, especially porch lights!

Ladybug - The Ladybug is a member of the Beetle family and comes in many different colors. The bright colors ac- tually warn predators to stay away. The wings of a Ladybug are neatly folded underneath its protective shell that will open when the ladybug spreads its wings!!

Moth - The Moth is a group of insects related to the Butterfly. Similar to the butterfly it begins its short life cycle as a caterpillar and emerges from a cocoon. Despite the fact that moths do not have noses, they are excellent sniffers and can detect some smells up to 7 miles away!

Slug - A Slug is similar to a snail, except it has no shell. It is believed that originally slugs lived in the ocean, which is why slugs need to stay moist. Slugs are gooey and sticky and leave a trail of slime wherever they go.

As a young girl, growing up in Framingham Massachusetts, Sheila loved to write and share creative verse and whimsical poems with her family and friends.

Now, many years later, and after a long career on Wall Street, Real Estate and local and county politics, Sheila has turned once again to her favorite pastime of story telling through poetry.

She and her husband Tom live in Tuckahoe New York and together have 4 children. She hopes that all of her readers enjoy her books as much as she enjoyed creating them.

Other Titles by Sheila

The Day That I Went to the Zoo

My Grandma Has a Garden

My Grandpa Has a Tool Bench

There is a Poem Inside of Me

The Jester and the King

The Flora and the Fauna

And more to come!

www.ingramcontent.com/pod-product-compliance
Lightning Source LLC
Chambersburg PA
CBHW051312020426
42333CB00027B/3303